Used in the enameling process, where glass frit and copper shapes become one, a sheet of mica is used as a tray and can withstand kiln temperatures up to 1700°F. Working on a particularly difficult piece, awaiting the peak melting point of the latest enameled creation, I wondered, "If mica doesn't melt in the kiln, what would happen if it were used with embossing powder?" It only took a moment to find out, and the results have forever changed how I do artwork. Connecting more dots, I also understood that the mica sheets, pulverized and colored, were indeed the same as the mica powdered pigments I used for my other artwork. They were a natural choice for use together!

After determining that mica sheets and block more closely resembled an irregularly shaped tile, I packaged the product, calling them Mica Tiles. In addition, we named the mica flakes and powders Perfect fx. That was nearly eight years ago, and the rest, as they say, is history.

Today avid Perfect fx and Mica Tile artisans from every field have also discovered the unlimited potential of mica – both as a canvas for artwork, and becoming the artwork itself, offering a natural and organic quality difficult to achieve with man-made or manufactured materials. Even a novice can paint on, stamp on, tear, cut and shape Mica Tiles. They are used as windows and methods for encapsulation in altered art projects, scrapbooking and cardmaking. Mica's ability to withstand high temperatures also makes it suitable for functional sculpture, such as lamps, screens and luminaries.

The flakes themselves, irregular and organically shaped, are easily dyed, sprinkled, heated and otherwise creatively tortured, all the while becoming the perfect effect for artwork, generously bestowing upon it gorgeous shots of natural light and sparkle.

While mica may be readily available in your own backyard or as lacquered laminated sheets produced for the electrical and lampshade-making industries, USArtQuest has led the way in bringing natural mica to the art, craft and interior design marketplaces. The ideas shown in this book provide just a few of the uses and methods for including mica in your next creative project.

Susan Pickering Rothamel

relatively soft and can be hand-cut, machine or die-cut. It is flexible, elastic and tough, noncombustible and non-flammable. In fact, its exceptional properties and resistance to heat make it virtually irreplaceable by any other material. Quite simply, mica is one of the most important insulation materials in the electrical industry. So great too, that no substitute, artificial or natural, has proven to be more economically suitable to replace it as "glass" windows in stove and kerosene heaters or as decorative panels in lamps and windows.

While subtle in color and virtually transparent, even when quite thick, both the ruby and green mica can also be found with interestingly patterned vegetable and mineral stained inclusions, borne through millions of years of crystalline development.

This 'stained' mica, while considered less desirable in some commercial applications, is also the very thing that makes it more desirable in the art industry. The inclusions offer projects a natural organic look, one that does not appear synthetic or manufactured.

The name phlogopite comes from the Greek word "phlogopos", which means "fire-like", referring to its red-brown color. It is much softer and lighter in weight than muscovite and this makes it more suitable for the remanufacturing into layered sheets for use in the electrical industry and as lampshades.

Mica occurs naturally in sheets called block, or in flakes called schist. Scrap mica, processed by breaking and grinding it into very small flakes and pieces, resembles schist. This is a slow, costly and extremely complicated process, because the mica is tough, having a plate-like structure. Meticulous care and precautions, taken during this process, prohibit the deterioration of its natural brilliance and color. While naturally occurring in dozens of natural colors, enhancing mica by calcining (heating) or coloring it synthetically occurs frequently in the plastics industry.

General Information When Using Mica Tiles

Many Pieces from One

Delamination of a Mica Tile

Mica, being many layers compressed by the millennia, is easily 'delaminated' but unable to be restored, except by artificial means. By slipping a fingernail or pointed tool into the edge of a Mica Tile, and then gently persuading it to come apart, many thinner layers come from a single piece.

If the layers become too thin, they lose their natural color and quality, resembling clear plastic. In addition, they may become too flimsy for many techniques.

The thinnest layers however, become very pretty when layered as fragments or as inclusions in collage or assemblage artwork. For many techniques, the piece should be just rigid enough that it does not bend easily without cracking.

Attaching Mica

Mechanical Devices

Nearly anything will work to attach two pieces of mica or more together. These encapsulated roses, sandwiched between two pieces of mica, are attached to the cardstock by one of several methods, including buttons, brads, decorative paper clips, stitching and eyelets.

Adhesives

To adhere two tiles together without using mechanical means, one must keep in mind that the mica is a rock and unable to accommodate the evaporative process easily, taking hours or even days for the clarity to reappear.

Therefore, sparingly use a lightweight, quality gloss adhesive only. Use enough to adhere, but not so much that it is too wet inside. In addition, specialty adhesives, such as Duo Embellishing Adhesive, Great Tape and other non-cellophane carrying tapes, will work for some techniques.

Foil Tape

Line up the two pieces of mica and run foil tape around the edges to give it a stained-glass window effect.

Finishing

When using Mica Tiles on furniture or other areas that might experience harder wear and tear, coat the finished project with one or more coats of gloss non-yellowing polyurethane to provide a protective finish. Work in a small area, or on a test area at first, to make sure the polyurethane performs properly.

Pinata fx

by Susan Pickering Rothamel

MATERIALS: *USArtQuest* (Perfect fx Mica Flakes, PPA-Gloss) • *Jacquard* (Piñata Colors, Extender) • Plastic bag • Waxed paper • Jars • Costume jewelry • Beads

INSTRUCTIONS: Select several different sized and colored mica flakes. Place a pinch of each into a little plastic bag. • Drizzle in a few drops of Piñata ink. • To achieve a more pastel effect, add a few drops of extender. For a more intense color, add more ink. • Swoosh around the ink and flakes in the bag, until all of the flakes are covered. • Dump the flakes onto a piece of waxed paper and let them dry thoroughly.• Store dried flakes in jars. • Decorate jar lids with beads, jewelry, and inks as desired.

Heart Art

by Julia Davenport

MATERIALS: *USArtQuest* (Perfect fx Mica Flakes-Stardust Small, Gold Folia cardstock, 101 Artist's Cement-Light, Tinz Heart, Great Tape, PPA, Excel board: Gold, White) • *Jacquard* Piñata (Extender, Colors: Senorita Magenta, Santa Fe Red, Passion Purple) • *Bazzill* cardstock (Bisque, Glossy White, Gold) • *Krylon* Gold leafing pen • Gold foil tape • Palette Knife • Sponge • Star buttons • Pearl costume jewelry

INSTRUCTIONS: **Cutting**: Cut Gold Excel board 5 3/4" x 5 3/4" and 2 1/2" x 2 1/2", Bisque cardstock 5 1/2" x 5 1/2" and 3 1/4" x 3 1/4", Gold cardstock 4 3/4" x 4 3/4", Glossy White cardstock 4 1/2" x 4 1/2" and 2 7/8" x 2 7/8", White Excel board 3 1/4" x 3 1/4". • **Marble technique**: Dab leafing pen on glossy cardstock. Drip Piñata Colors over cardstock. Move color around with a sponge. Do one color at a time to keep the colors from getting muddy. Allow the colors to run together. Let dry. • **Matting**: Add Gold foil tape around the edge of the small Gold Excel board. Use PPA to glue the mats together in the following order from the bottom: Gold Excel board, Bisque, Gold cardstock, Marbled, White Excel board covered with Bisque cardstock, Marbled, Gold with foil edging. • **Pearls**: Color the costume jewelry with Piñata inks. Let dry. • **Heart**: Cover heart with 101 using a palette knife. Make sure the 101 is at least 1/8" thick. Press in pearls and star buttons. Sprinkle on Perfect fx to cover the 101 between the pearls. • Adhere heart with PPA.

Perfect Effects

Piñata fx are made from glistening bits of mica and permanent inks. They are created to be used when a more colorful, yet natural look is desired. Make these colorful elements in advance and save them in pretty jars so they will be ready to use in a moment's notice.

Use jars with tight-fitting wooden tops. Coat the lids with inks and top with jewelry crowns to match each jar.

1. Place a pinch of mica flakes in a plastic bag. Drizzle in a few drops of ink.

2. Mix the ink and flakes until all of the flakes are covered.

3. Dry mica flakes on paper.

General Information About Forms of Mica

Stained Mica Tiles

For a lighter stained appearance, simply thin the mica. Each subsequent thinning will reduce the amount of stain, with each layer displaying less of the splattering and crosshatch patterning.

Mica Flakes, Granules, Powders and Colors

Scrap and flake mica, produced all over the world, can also be found in Arizona, North Carolina, South Dakota, Georgia, New Mexico and South Carolina. North Carolina's production alone, accounts for half of the total U.S. mica production. Canada, India, Finland and Japan also export flake mica to the U.S. Sheet or block mica is considerably less abundant than flake and scrap mica.

In the U.S., sheet mica is only recovered from mining scrap and flake mica in limited quantities. However, abundant mica deposits in India, Africa, Brazil and China supply most of the world's mica needs.

Mica Flakes

Mica Chips

Mica Powder

Natural Pearl Flakes

Natural Bronze Powder

Mica Schist

Mica Calcined

Mica Artificially Colored

Through the Looking Glass

by Susan Pickering Rothamel

MATERIALS: *USArtQuest* (Mica Tiles-Grand Effects, All colors of Perfect fx Mica Flakes, 101 Artist's Cement-Heavy, PPA) • *Jacquard* Piñata Colors • Stencil • Old book • Palette knife

INSTRUCTIONS: **Covers**: Cut the front and back covers from the book, leaving all of the bound edge. • **Mica**: Cut mica to fit covers. Adhere mica behind the book cover edge with 101. • Use PPA to adhere the title page to the mica on the front cover. Place another piece of mica over the title page. • **Binding**: Lay stencil on the binding. Apply 101 through the stencil with a palette knife. Carefully lift the stencil and fill in any spaces in the pattern. Sprinkle with mica flakes. Let dry.

Picture Frame

by Susan Pickering Rothamel

MATERIALS: *USArtQuest* (Mica Tiles-Extra Large or Grand Effects, Perfect fx Mica Flakes, Gossamer paper, 101 Artist's Cement-Heavy, PPA) • Hole punch • 4 *Chatterbox* tacks • 2 large eyelets • 2 dowels • Fine gauge wire • Stencil • Palette knife • Dragonfly cut-out

INSTRUCTIONS: **Mica**: Place 2 Mica Tiles together, either lining them up, or skewing the top piece. Hold them firmly to the table and punch 4 holes for snaps. Use tacks to fasten the 2 pieces together. • **Dowels**: Cut 2 dowels 7 1/2" long. Paint if desired. Securely wire dowels together as shown. • Set eyelets large enough for the dowel ends to slide through. Place them near the bottom of the joined pieces as shown. • **Embellishments**: Use a palette knife to smooth 101 through the stencil. Immediately sprinkle on Perfect fx. Clean the stencil and continue randomly placing the design. • Cover the dragonfly with 101 and Perfect fx. Curl the wings and tail. Let dry. Wrap the tail and body with wire, curling the wire ends for antennae. Adhere dragonfly to mica with PPA. • **Finish**: Slide the dowels into place. • Back a photo with Gossamer paper. Remove a tack to open the mica sandwich. Slide a photo between the top and bottom layers of mica. Replace the tack.

Sparkling Stenciling for Dazzling Effects

This unique photo frame is sure to catch anyone's eye. It is easy to remove a snap and change the photo.

Layered Mica Tiles bring a new dimension to altered books. Mica can be attached using 101, punched holes, wire, eyelets, brads or screws.

1. Punch the holes in the mica.

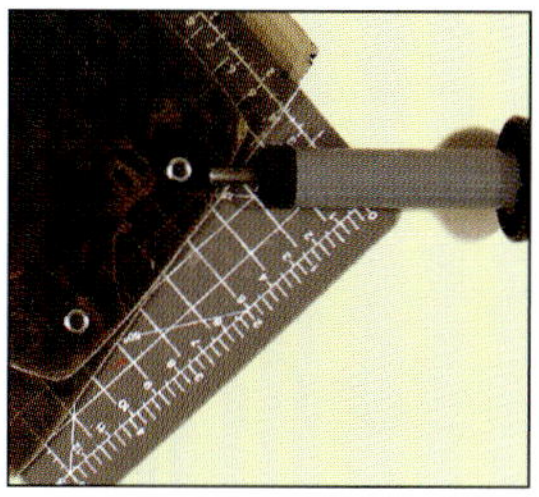

2. Set eyelets.

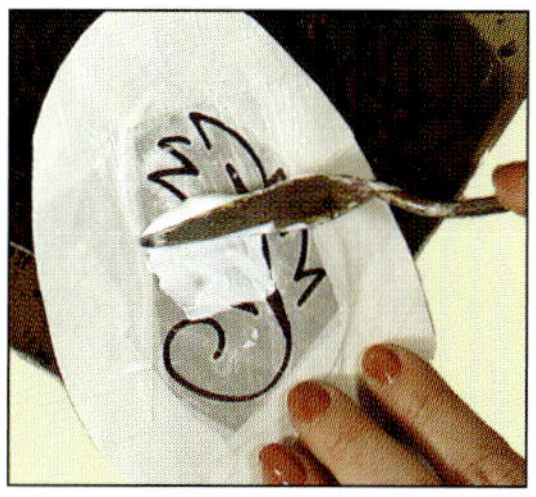

3. Use a palette knife to smooth Artist's Cement on the stencil.

4. Sprinkle on the Perfect fx.

5. Slide the easel into place.

Mica, being organic in nature, easily passes as shining rock surfaces, especially when incorporated into a scenic collage.

Collage Art

by Susan Pickering Rothamel

MATERIALS: *USArtQuest* (Mica Tiles, Perfect fx Mica Flakes, Gildenglitz (Variegated), Copper Excel matboard, Great Tape, PPA-Gloss, Duo Adhesive, Texture sponge, Folia cardstock: Black, Tan, White) • *Hero Arts* Leaf stamp • Embossing powder (Black, Gold) • *Suze Weinberg* UTEE • *Tsukineko* Versamark ink pad • Decorative papers

INSTRUCTIONS: **Mat**: Cut a triple mat of Copper, Black, and Tan. Tape mats together. • Cut a rectangle of matboard to fit on top of the mat. • **Collage**: Adhere papers and mica flakes to the matboard with PPA. Let dry. • Remove the Great Tape from the roll and twist it around the edges to form a border. Sprinkle mica flakes. Emboss with UTEE in one or both colors. • Cover a piece of White cardstock with Duo Adhesive. Let dry until clear and tacky. Apply Gildenglitz. Burnish with a sponge. Stamp leaves on gilding with Versamark ink. Emboss with Black. Cut out leaves. • Stamp some mica pieces with Versamark ink and emboss with Gold. • Adhere mica sheets, mica flakes glitter, and leaves with PPA • **Finish**: Tape matboard to mat.

Daisy Card

by Julia Davenport

MATERIALS: *USArtQuest* (Mica, Gildenglitz: Summer Splendor, Great Tape, Sandi Miller Art Stamps, Duo Adhesive, Texture sponge, Folia cardstock: Red, Mustard, Black) • *Ranger* Cut n' Dry • Black embossing powder • Heat gun • Black ink pad

INSTRUCTIONS: **Card**: Cut Red cardstock 5" x 10". Fold in half to 5" x 5". **Mat**: Cut a Mustard mat $4^1/2$" x $4^1/2$". Stamp Daisies with Black ink. Glue to card. • Cut a Red mat 4" x 4". Glue to card. • **Mica mat**: Fold a thin piece of mica, first in one direction, then the other, to make fractures in a uniform pattern. Cut a $3^3/4$" square. Tape to card. • **Top design**: Cut Black mat $3^1/4$" square. Apply Duo to mat. Let dry. After it turns clear and tacky, apply Gildenglitz. Burnish with a sponge. • Stamp with Duo applied to the Cut n' Dry pad. Emboss with Black. Tape to card.

1. Accordion pleat a thin square of mica.

Shell Card

by Frankie Fioretti

Fractured mica shards effectively mimic glistening water when used with seascape imagery.

MATERIALS: *USArtQuest* (Mica Tiles, Mica Flakes, 101 Artist's Cement, Great Tape, Sandi Miller Art Stamps, Folia cardstock: Blue, White, Turquoise) • Seashells • *Krylon* Gold Leafing pen • Embossing powder (Green, Blue) • Gold Pigment ink • *Jacquard* (Baja Blue Piñata Colors, Lumiere paint: Dark Blues, Greens) • Sponge • Paintbrush • Heat gun

INSTRUCTIONS: **Card**: Cut Blue cardstock $5^{1}/_{8}$" x $9^{1}/_{2}$". Fold in half to $4^{3}/_{4}$" x $5^{1}/_{8}$". Stamp with Gold ink. • Cut a Blue mat $4^{1}/_{8}$" x $4^{7}/_{8}$". Paint with Lumiere. Add dots of Gold leafing. Let dry. Use a ruler to edge with Gold leafing pen. Glue to card. • Cut a Turquoise mat $3^{1}/_{4}$" x $4^{1}/_{8}$". Edge with Gold. Glue to card. • Cut a White cardstock 3" x $3^{3}/_{4}$". Sponge the middle with Baja Blue paint. Let dry. Glue to card. • **Mica**: Paint 101 on Mica Tile. While wet, sprinkle mica flakes and small pieces of mica. Add small pieces of very thin mica. Add Blue and Green embossing powder. Heat. Adhere seashells and glue mica to card with 101.

Butterfly Card

by Susan Pickering Rothamel

MATERIALS: *USArtQuest* (Mica, Gossamer paper, Parchment paper, Gold Excel board, Stargazer Watercolor Palette, Great Tape, PPA, Detail brush, Sandi Miller Art Stamps: Butterfly) • *Krylon* Gold Leafing pen • *Hasbro* Miniature Scrabble Letters • *Bazzill* cardstock (White, Mauve) • Gold embossing powder • *Tsukineko* Versamark ink pad • *Fiskars* Scissors • Ruler

INSTRUCTIONS: **Card**: Fold an 8" x 10" sheet of Mauve cardstock in half 5" x 8". • Cut a sheet of Gold Excel board 4" x $6^{1}/_{2}$". Glue to card. • Cut a Parchment paper mat $3^{3}/_{4}$" x $6^{1}/_{4}$". Glue to card.• **Butterfly**: Stamp the butterfly image on heavy White cardstock. Emboss with Gold. Color the butterfly sections with pearlescent, metallic, or glistening watercolors. Cut out the butterfly and bend its wings upwards, from the edge of the body. Use your fingers to gently shape the wings into a curve. • **Mica**: Thin a sheet of mica big enough to cover part of the card front. Tear the mica, deliberately fracturing the mica shard creating a torn mica edge. • **Assembly**: Adhere Gossamer paper to card. Adhere mica over Gossamer with PPA. Tape the body of the butterfly to the mica, allowing the wings to stand up. Paint Scrabble letters with Pink watercolors. Let dry. Glue letters to card.

1. Stamp image. Emboss in Gold. Color image.

2. Cut out butterfly. Bend the wings upwards. Gently shape wings into a curve.

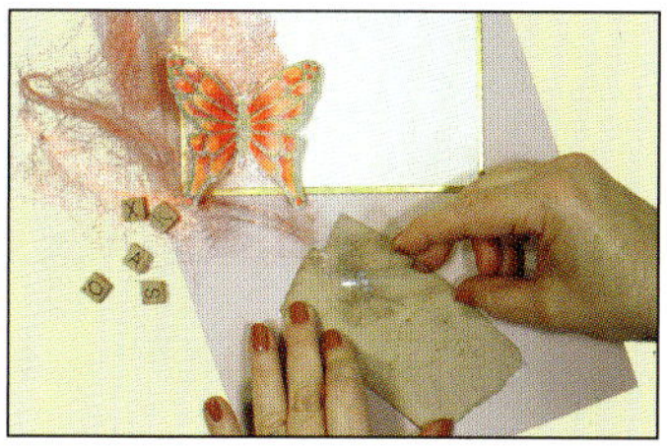

3. Tear thinned mica creating a torn-mica edge.

4. Adhere butterfly and papers to parchment.

Stamping on Sparkling Mica

Daisy Card

by Frankie Fioretti

The embossed dragonfly on mica adds a lovely accent and translucent sparkle to this bright daisy card.

MATERIALS: *USArtQuest* (Mica Tiles, Sandi Miller Art Stamps, PPA, Great Tape) • *Krylon* Gold Leafing Pen • *Jacquard* Piñata Colors • Cardstock (Burgundy, Glossy White, Brown) • Black embossing powder • *Tsukineko* Versamark ink pad • Ruler • Sponge

INSTRUCTIONS: **Card**: Cut Burgundy cardstock 5 1/2" x 8 1/2". Fold in half to 4 1/4" x 5 1/2". Cut Glossy cardstock 4" x 5 1/4". Set aside for marbling. • Cut a 3" Burgundy square. Cut a 2 7/8" Brown square. Cut a 2 3/8" White glossy square. • **Marbling**: Drizzle the Gold, Red, Green and Orange inks onto the large glossy cardstock. Let dry. Ink the edge with Gold leafing pen.• Sponge a darker square in the center of the small glossy cardstock. Sponge a Green border around the dark square. Let dry. Ink the edge with Gold leafing pen. • **Daisy**: Stamp the daisy in Versamark ink. Emboss in Black. Color with Piñata ink. • **Mica**: Stamp the dragonfly in Versamark ink. Emboss in Black. Color back of mica with Piñata inks. • **Assembly**: Glue large marbled cardstock to the card. Tape mica to card. • Layer the 3" Burgundy square, Brown square, and Daisy square. Adhere layers to card with tape.

Leaf Card

by Sandi Miller

Nearly everything looks terrific on a crackled background, especially natural things like this leaf.

MATERIALS: *USArtQuest* (Mica, White Gossamer Paper, PPA-Gloss, Great Tape, 101 Craze and Crackle, Sandi Miller Art Stamps, Folia cardstock: Black, Orange) • *Jacquard* Piñata Colors • *Krylon* Gold Leafing Pen • Gold embossing powder • *Tsukineko* Versamark ink pad • 4 eyelets • Eyelet tools • Palette knife • Sponge

INSTRUCTIONS: **Card**: Cut Black cardstock 6" x 9". Fold in half to 4 1/2" x 6". Cut Orange cardstock 4 1/4" x 5 3/4", glue to the card. Cut a Black mat 3 1/4" x 4 1/2". • **Crackle**: Cut a Black mat 3" x 4 1/4". Apply Crackle paste to mat with a palette knife. Let dry. Sponge Piñata inks over crackled mat. Let dry. Edge with Gold leafing pen. Attach crackle to Black mat. • **Assembly:** Adhere Gossamer to card. Glue Crackle mat to card. • **Mica**: Stamp leaf with Versamark on Mica. Emboss with Gold. Edge mica with Gold leafing pen. Adhere mica to card with PPA.

Skeleton Leaf Journal

by Frankie Fioretti

This little journal fits neatly into a purse or sits prettily on your desk. It would also be a great gift for a special friend.

MATERIALS: *USArtQuest* (Mica Tile, Perfect fx Mica Flakes, Skeleton Leaf, PPA-Gloss, Sandi Miller Art Stamps) • 2" square *Ranger* Cut n' Dry foam ink pad • *Jacquard* (Black Lumiere paint, Piñata Colors, Piñata Extender) • *Krylon* Gold Leafing Pen • Paper scraps (Mulberry, handmade) • Matboard • Pad of paper • Paintbrush

INSTRUCTIONS: **Mica**: Apply Black paint to the Cut n' Dry pad. Use the pad to ink the stamp. Stamp onto a thinned Mica Tile. Let dry. • Turn the stamped Mica Tile over and drip the inks onto the backside. Let dry. • **Ink**: Drip inks onto the matboard for the journal covers, the skeleton leaf, and a cardstock rectangle smaller than the cover. Use several harmonious colors, blending the edges with extender. Let dry. • **Journal Covers**: Sandwich the pad of paper between the 2 inked matboard covers. Glue them to the top and bottom page of the pad. Cut a binding from the soft paper. Adhere it to the top of the journal and both covers with PPA. • **Decorations**: Edge the inked rectangle with Gold. Adhere it to the front cover. Tear a piece of handmade paper and glue it in place. Adhere the leaf and mica. Glue some mica flakes to the lower front of the notebook.

Aruba Scrapbook Page

by Julia Davenport

These large fractured mica pieces look just like a school of fish in the cool ocean reefs off Aruba. The "Vacation memories" journaling was printed and transferred directly to the page using Studio Paper.

MATERIALS: *USArtQuest* (Mica Tiles, Perfect fx Mica Flakes, Gold Excel matboard, Studio Paper, PPA-Gloss, PPA-Matte, Great Tape) • Stamps (*Stampa Rosa, Fred Mullet*) • *K & Company* paper (Marbled paper, Tan cardstock) • *Mrs. Grossman's* stickers "Aruba" • *Jacquard* Lumiere (Metallic Olive, Black) • *Ranger* Cut n' Dry • Paper crimper

INSTRUCTIONS: **Background**: Stamp reeds on the bottom of the page with Lumiere and Cut n' Dry. Let dry. • Use PPA to adhere mica flakes to the page. • **Photo**: Cut a Marbled paper mat 5 1/2" x 7 1/2". Cut Gold matboard 4 1/2" x 6 3/4". Cut Tan cardstock 4 1/4" x 6 1/2". Crimp it. Mat photo as shown. • **Journaling**: Set your inkjet printer on the highest quality setting. Print a mirror image of your words on Studio Paper. Do Not run Studio Paper thru a laser or toner copier/printer! Allow a few minutes for some of the moisture on the copy to evaporate before transferring the image. Place Studio Paper on cardstock. Burnish carefully until the letters are completely adhered to the cardstock. • **Mica**: Stamp fish on the back of the Mica Tiles. Let dry. Adhere Mica Tiles and flakes to page with PPA-Gloss. • **Title**: Adhere title stickers.

Thinking of You Card

by Frankie Fioretti

Mica is very strong. You can punch holes in it with any hand-held punch. This makes it easy for you to attach mica to your projects with eyelets or brads.

MATERIALS: *USArtQuest* (Mica Tile, Perfect fx Mica Flakes, PPA, Sandi Miller Art Stamps, Tan Folia cardstock) • *Lasting Impressions* (Brads, Papers: Printed, Assorted colors mulberry, White handmade) • Dried flower • Black embossing powder • *Tsukineko* Versamark ink pad • Hole punch

INSTRUCTIONS: **Card**: Cut Tan cardstock 6 1/2" x 10". Fold in half to 5" x 6 1/2". Cut printed paper mat 4 1/2" x 6". Glue to card with PPA. • **Collage**: Cut White mat 4" x 5 1/2". • Tear assorted mulberry papers Adhere mulberry paper and flowers to mat with PPA. • **Mica**: Stamp and emboss "Thinking of You" on the mica. Punch holes in the mica. Attach tile to White mat with brads. • Adhere mat to card with PPA. Add mica flakes.

Collage Card

by Frankie Fioretti

A Mica Tile stamped with Lumiere and embellished with mica flakes looks great on a collaged paper background.

MATERIALS: *USArtQuest* (Mica Tile, PPA, Folia cardstock: Ecru, White) • *Jacquard* Copper Lumiere • Decorative papers (Printed script, Assorted colors mulberry, White handmade) • Dried Brown leaf

INSTRUCTIONS: **Card**: Cut Ecru cardstock 6 1/2" x 10". Fold in half to 5" x 6 1/2". Cut Script mat 4 1/4" x 6". Glue to card with PPA. • **Collage**: Cut White paper 4" x 5 3/4". • Tear assorted mulberry papers to form sky and ground. Adhere to paper with PPA. Adhere leaf. • Paint Copper Lumiere onto stamp. Stamp on Mica Tile. Let dry. Adhere mica flakes to the bottom corner of collage. Adhere mica to collage and glue collage to card with PPA.

How to Make a Leaf Journal

1. Stamp onto the thinned Mica Tile. Let dry.

2. Apply inks to the leaf, matboard and back of the mica.

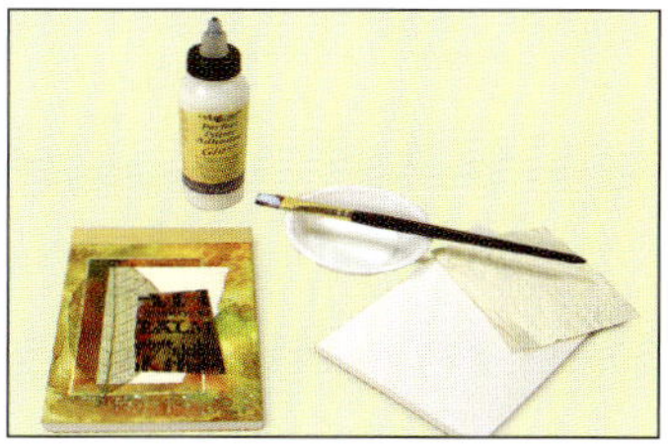

3. Adhere binding to the top of the journal and both of the covers.

Mica Die-Cuts: Transparent Shapes

1. Cut the Mica Tile to fit the die.

2. Use die-cuts to cut mica. Use the negative spaces in projects too! You can also punch holes with a hand-held punch.

3. Color die-cut mica with ink. Let dry. Spray webbing on piece.

4. Edge the windows and sides with a Silver leafing pen.

4 o'clock

by Susan Pickering Rothamel

This little collage art is the result of using both squares and the negative window shape left after die-cutting the squares.

Add dimension to your frame pieces by gluing clear vinyl buttons to the back of the mica frame.

MATERIALS: *USArtQuest* (Mica, PPA-Gloss, Great Tape, Excel matboard: Gold, Black) • White handmade paper with embedded mica flakes • *AccuCut* die-cut • *Memory Makers* Numbers • *Krylon* (White Webbing Spray, Silver Leafing pen) • Watch parts • Clear vinyl buttons • Printed paper • Red cardstock • Permanent ink • Cotton swab

INSTRUCTIONS: **Mat**: Cut Gold matboard 6 1/2" x 8". Cut Black matboard 6" x 7 1/2". Cut printed paper 5 1/4" x 6 1/2". Cut Red cardstock 4 1/2" x 5 1/2". Tear handmade paper slightly smaller than the Red mat. • Tape all the layers together. • **Mica**: Cut mica to fit die-cut. Cut mica shapes. • Color the die-cut shapes with ink. Let it dry. Spray the webbing onto the piece. • Edge the windows and sides with a Silver leafing pen. • Use PPA to glue the clear vinyl buttons to the underside of the mica and to adhere mica to the handmade paper. • **Embellishments**: Adhere paper to the back of 4 mica squares. • Color the Copper numbers with ink and a cotton swab. Add bits of Silver with a leafing pen. Adhere the numbers to the mica squares. Adhere mica squares and watch parts with PPA.

Life with Twins Scrapbook Page

by Frankie Fioretti

Using die-cut mica daisies as embellishments and photos corners takes advantage of the transparency of the mica, allowing the paper pattern to show through.

MATERIALS: *USArtQuest* (Mica Tiles, Great Tape) • *Doodlebug Designs* paper • *Making Memories* Green flower brads • *Li'l Davis Designs* (Stickers, Quick Quotes) • *Ellison* (Die-cut machine, rectangle die, flower dies) • *McGill* hole punch • Eyelets • Eyelet tools

INSTRUCTIONS: **Photos**: Cut mats with rectangle die. Mat photos on 2 coordinating papers. Add sticker letters. Adhere to page. • **Journaling**: Adhere "Quick Quotes Life with Twins" to page. • **Mica**: Thin mica and cut it to fit the die. Cut out flowers. • Punch holes in the center of each flower. Adhere flowers to page with eyelets and brads.

You Met Me

by Frankie Fioretti

These mini goldfish are so cute. Adhere them to a card especially made for a friend or the love of your life.

MATERIALS: *USArtQuest* (Mica Tiles, Stargazer Watercolor Palette, Interference Watercolor Palette, White Folia cardstock, PPA-Gloss, Great Tape) • *Jacquard* Piñata colors • Paintbrush • *AccuCut* die-cuts • Vellum • Turquoise brads • Dry embossing tool • Ruler

INSTRUCTIONS: **Card**: Cut White cardstock 6" x 8 1/2". Fold in half to 4 1/4" x 6". • **Watercolor paper**: Cut White cardstock mat 3 3/4" x 5 1/2". Wet paintbrush. Dip in Blue/Green color. Wash brush across paper to create a marbled effect. Let dry. • **Vellum**: Print words on vellum. Cut vellum to fit card. Attach vellum to watercolor paper with brads. Tape to card. • **Frame**: Cut White cardstock 2 1/2" x 2 3/4". Dry emboss a square 1/4" inside the outer edge of the square. Color the inside square with Pearlescent watercolors and a wet brush. Let dry. Glue frame in place. • **Mica**: Thin the mica. Die-cut the fish. Adhere to card with PPA.

Goldfish Card

by Frankie Fioretti

Frankie used both a fish die-cut and circles that look much like bubbles. Colored from the back, just like the 'Stamping on Mica' project, the fish is swimming across sea blue paper.

MATERIALS: *USArtQuest* (Mica Tiles, Gossamer Paper, Stargazer Watercolor Palette, White Folia cardstock, PPA-Gloss, Detail paintbrush) • *AccuCut* die-cuts • *Jacquard* Piñata colors • 1/4" hole punch • Dry embossing tool • Ruler • Sponge

INSTRUCTIONS: **Card**: Cut White cardstock 7" x 10". Fold in half to 5" x 7". • Dry emboss a rectangle 3/4" from each edge of the card. • **Mat**: Cut a White cardstock mat 3" x 5". Use a wet paintbrush to swirl watercolors in a marbled pattern. Let dry. Glue mat in the center of the embossed rectangle. • **Mica**: Thin mica and trim it to fit die. Cut out fish and circles. • Sponge the back of the mica with Piñata colors. Let dry. • **Finish**: Adhere Gossamer paper, mica fish, circles, and flakes with PPA.

Mica Die-Cuts:
Transparent Shapes

Die-cutting is fun and easy, only requiring access to numerous dies and the machine. Punches or hole punches, come in dozens of shapes, sizes and patterns. The trick is to keep the mica thin and still be large enough to fill the die shape.

Mica Encapsulation: Creative Window Dressing

Flowers and Leaves

by Frankie Fioretti

Pressed flowers adhered to a small piece of cardstock look stunning under this corner-punched Mica Tile.

MATERIALS: *USArtQuest* (Mica Tile, Gildenglitz foil, PPA, Brush, Sandi Miller Art Stamps) • Cardstock (Manila, Black) • Gold thread • Corner punch • Mauve pigment ink • Dried flowers
INSTRUCTIONS: **Card**: Cut Manila cardstock 4 1/4" x 8 1/2". Fold in half to 4 1/4" x 4 1/4". Stamp card with leaves. Cut a 2 1/4" Black square mat. Glue to card. • **Mica**: Make a mica/flower sandwich adding Gildenglitz. Cut a 3 1/4" mica square. Punch the corners. Wrap Gold thread around the corners. Adhere mica to card with PPA.

Collage Card

by Frankie Fioretti

These projects will inspire you to gather and dry the wildflowers in your yard. Because mica is a natural material, it enhances the beauty of any botanical.

MATERIALS: *USArtQuest* (Mica Tile, Mica Flakes, White Folia cardstock, PPA-Gloss, Brush, Sandi Miller Art Stamps) • Mulberry papers • Pigment ink (Green, Purple) • Dried flowers INSTRUCTIONS: **Card**: Cut White cardstock 10" x 6 1/2". Fold in half to 5" x 6 1/2". Tear the bottom edge of the front of the card.• Adhere mulberry papers to card, creating a scenic motif. Consider placements of the paper to include a "middle ground" and background. The mica will become the foreground. • Stamp flowers in the "middle ground" of the card. **Mica**: Make a mica/flower sandwich. • Run trails of PPA along the bottom of the card, sprinkling mica flakes all along the way. • Adhere the pressed flower mica piece to the card with gloss PPA and add a few more trails of mica flakes over the bottom edge.

How to Make a Mica/Flower Sandwich

Select a piece of mica and thin it into 2 pieces. Adhere pressed flowers to one half of the Mica Tile with gloss PPA. Let dry. • Brush a very light coat of PPA on the other piece of mica. Place it over the flowers, making a mica and flower sandwich. Use only enough adhesive to hold the mica together.

1. Adhere art papers to cardstock, creating a scenic motif.

2. Glue mica sandwich together.

3. Glue mica flakes to the bottom edge of the card.

A Rose Is A ... *by Frankie Fioretti*

Inspired by a British friend, this card is sewn with thin copper wire. It is so pretty showing off the suspended encapsulated rose.

MATERIALS: *USArtQuest* (Mica Tile, PPA, Brush) • White cardstock • Decorative papers (Leaf print, Light Tan) • Thin Copper wire • Dried flowers • *Krylon* Gold Leafing pen • Dry embossing tool • Ruler • 1/16" hole punch • Tape

INSTRUCTIONS: **Card**: Cut Leaf paper 6 1/2" x 10". Fold in half to 5" x 6 1/2". • Cut Tan mat 4 1/2" x 6". Glue to card. • **White mat**: Cut White mat 4 1/4" x 5 3/4". Cut out a 2 1/2" x 3 3/4" window in the center of the mat. Dry emboss a rectangle 1/4" from the window edge. Punch holes 1/8" from the window edge. Use a ruler to trim the outer edge of the mat with Gold leafing pen.• **Mica**: Make a mica/flower sandwich. Punch holes around the edge of the mica to match the holes in the White mat. Sew mica to window with Copper wire. Tape wire ends to the back of the mat. • Glue mat to card.

Dream Card *by Frankie Fioretti*

Simply lovely! While the mica appears to be held by a single eyelet, it really is adhered from the underside with a gloss adhesive.

MATERIALS: *USArtQuest* (Mica Tile, PPA-Gloss, Brush) • Cardstock (Tan, White textured) • Decorative papers (Green print, Light Green solid) • *Making Memories* Rub-On "dream" • Dried leaf • White plastic disc • Brown eyelet • Eyelet tools • Dry embossing tool • Ruler

INSTRUCTIONS: **Card**: Cut Manila cardstock 6 3/4" x 9 1/2". Fold in half to 4 3/4" x 6 3/4". • **White mat**: Cut White textured mat 4 1/2" x 6 1/2". Dry emboss a 3/4" x 1 3/4" rectangle 1/2" above the bottom of the card. Adhere the "dream" Rub-On inside the embossed rectangle. Glue mat to card. • **Green mats**: Cut leaf patterned paper 3" x 4 1/4" and Light Green 2 1/2" x 3 3/4". Glue mats together. • **Mica**: Make a mica sandwich using the dried leaf. Adhere mica to Green mat. • **Finish**: Attach disc with eyelet. Glue matted mica to card.

Daisies & Lace *by Frankie Fioretti*

Queen Anne's Lace presses out nicely. Combine it with encapsulated daisies for a delightful handmade summertime card.

MATERIALS: *USArtQuest* (Mica Tile, Mica Flakes, Gildenglitz foil, PPA, Brush) • Tan cardstock • Tan Script decorative paper • White handmade paper • Mulberry papers • Dried flowers

INSTRUCTIONS: **Card**: Cut Tan cardstock 7" x 10". Fold in half to 5" x 7". Cut a Script mat 4 1/4" x 6". Cut a White mat 4" x 5 3/4". Glue mats to card. • **Collage**: Adhere Mulberry papers, Gildenglitz and dried Queen Anne's Lace with PPA. • **Mica**: Adhere mica flakes across the top of the card. Make a mica sandwich using the dried daisies. Adhere mica to card with PPA.

Creative photo transfers have never been so easy! Whether on mica or paper, this technique is a winner. Use transfers for cards, altered art and especially for those fun scrapbook pages.

Mica Transfers:

Transferring Images to Mica the Easy Way

Jill and Rose Scrapbook Page

by Julia Davenport and Susan Pickering Rothamel

MATERIALS: *USArtQuest* (Mica Tile-Large, Gossamer Paper, Skeleton leaves, Duo Embellishing Adhesive, Soft applicator, Studio Paper, Stargazer Watercolor Palette, Paintbrush, PPA) • *Susy Ratto* sticker letters • *Lasting Impressions* Pink brads • *Bo-Bunny Press* sticker words • *It Takes Two* paper • Cardstock (Lavender, White) • Photo • Die-cuts • Hole punch

INSTRUCTIONS: **Background**: Paint skeleton leaves Pink. Let dry. Adhere large Mica Tiles, skeleton leaves, and Gossamer paper to the page. Add stickers. • **Mica**: Transfer photo to Mica Tile. Tear Lavender cardstock to fit behind the mica. Watercolor the edges. Punch holes in mica. Adhere mica to torn Lavender with brads. Adhere matted mica to page. • **Flowers**: Die-cut flowers from White cardstock. Color with watercolors. Adhere to page.

How to Make a Mica Transfer

Mica: Peel the Mica Tile into at least two layers. One piece will take the transfer. The other will be coated with Duo Embellishing Adhesive. The Duo'ed piece will be adhered to the photo transferred Mica Tile. • **Printing**: Set your inkjet on the highest quality print setting. Print the image on Studio Paper using an inkjet printer or copier. DO NOT run Studio Paper thru a laser or toner copier/printer. Ink will not dry on Studio Paper. However, you will get a better result if you allow a few minutes for some of the moisture on the copy to evaporate before transferring the image. • **Transfer image**: Gently lay the non-Duo'ed Mica Tile onto the image. Burnish gently with a tissue. Carefully turn the tile and Studio Paper over, burnishing it gently from the back too. Carefully peel away the Studio Paper, leaving the image on the mica. Wipe off the Studio Paper for use on another transfer. • Dry the Mica Tile thoroughly. Speeding up the process with a heat gun is best. If the transfer is not dry, condensation will be trapped between the mica layers and will ruin the image. • **Adhesive**: Apply a very thin coat of Duo to the bottom Tile, and allow it to dry completely. • The best applicator is a delicately textured sponge or very soft wide brush. The applicator will determine the texture created by the Duo. A soft applicator yields less texture. A brush will provide more texture. When desiring less texture, allow the Duo to flow, applying it in random patterns, such as swirls, avoiding obvious strokes. • Avoid creating bubbles when applying the adhesive. • Allow the adhesive to dry naturally. Do Not use a heat gun. It makes a difference. • **Finish**: Carefully lay the Duo'ed tile onto the transferred image. For a very subtle image, mount the finished tile onto a medium value paper, such as Beige, Taupe or Gray. For a more distinct image, mount the tile onto a light colored or subtle patterned surface. This will enhance the image.

1. Copy image onto Studio Paper using an inkjet printer or copier. Let dry.

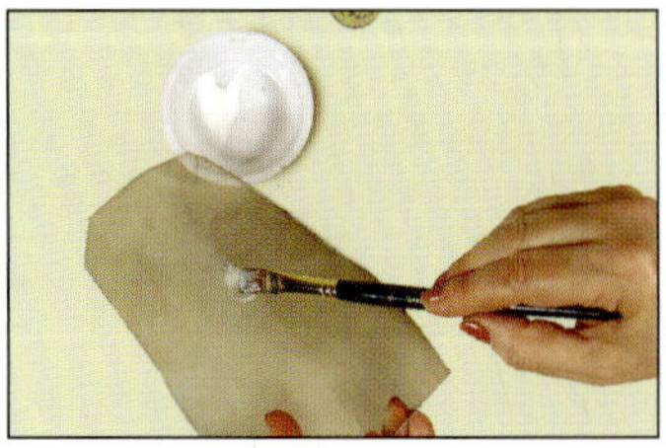

2. Brush a thin coat of Duo on the bottom tile. Let dry.

3. Gently lay the non-Duo'ed Mica Tile onto the image. Burnish gently with a tissue.

4. Carefully turn over. Gently burnish the back.

Tips for Successful Transfers:
• A photo with greater contrast will transfer more clearly. This is why old black and white photographs work very well. Select color photographs with the greatest color contrast, such as a blue sky against dark trees or people. • Don't forget - Words must be printed in mirror image for transferring. • You must use an inkjet copier or printer and Studio Paper. Do not use a laser or toner printer/copier.

Happy Mother's Day
by Frankie Fioretti

MATERIALS: *USArtQuest* (Mica Tile, PPA, Duo Embellishing Adhesive, Soft applicator, Studio Paper, Folia cardstock: Rose, White) • Papers (*Penny Black, Anna Griffin*) • *Jolee's Boutique* flower stickers • *Krylon* Gold Leafing pen

INSTRUCTIONS: **Card**: Cut Rose cardstock 6 1/2" x 12". Fold in half to 6" x 6 1/2". • Cut printed paper mat 5 3/4" x 6 1/4". Glue to card. • Cut embossed White paper 4 3/4" x 5 1/4". Edge with Gold leafing, adhere to card. • **Mica**: Transfer photo to mica. Adhere tile to card. • **Finish**: Print "Happy Mother's Day". Cut out words. Edge with Gold leafing. Adhere to card. Adhere flower stickers.

Nature's Beauty Journal
by Frankie Fioretti

MATERIALS: *USArtQuest* (Mica Tile, PPA-Gloss, Duo Embellishing Adhesive, Soft applicator, Studio Paper) • *Making Memories* Metal Words • Decorative papers (Yellow Marbled scrap, Mulberry paper, Tan watercolor scrap, Handmade paper) • Matboard for cover • Leaf stamp • Burgundy ink • Black waxed linen thread • Needle • 1/8" hole punch

INSTRUCTIONS: **Covers:** Cut 2 matboard covers 5" x 7 1/2" and 2 matboard book spines 1" x 7 1/2". Cover the matboards with torn handmade papers. • Lay the 1" strip beside the cover with 1/4" between. Cut a strip of Tan watercolor 1 1/2" x 7 1/2". Glue the cover and spine to the Tan paper. • **Inside papers**: Cut 12 pages 5" x 7 1/2" of handmade paper for the inside of the book • **Binding**: Mark and punch 5 holes in the spine and papers. Sew binding with Black thread. • **Decoration**: Adhere Mulberry and marbled papers to cover as desired. Stamp leaf near the bottom corner. Adhere metal word. • **Mica**: Transfer image to the mica. Adhere mica to front cover.

How to Make a Paper Transfer

Printing: Set your inkjet on the highest quality print setting. Remember to print the mirror image of all words. Print the image on Studio Paper using an inkjet printer or copier. DO NOT run Studio Paper thru a laser or toner copier/printer. Ink will not dry on Studio Paper. However, you will get a better result if you allow a few minutes for some of the moisture on the copy to evaporate before transferring the image. • **Transfer image**: Gently lay the image on the paper you wish to transfer to. Burnish gently with a tissue. Carefully turn over, burnishing it gently from the back too. Carefully peel away the Studio Paper, leaving the image on the page. Wipe off the Studio Paper for use on another transfer. • Let the transfer dry completely.

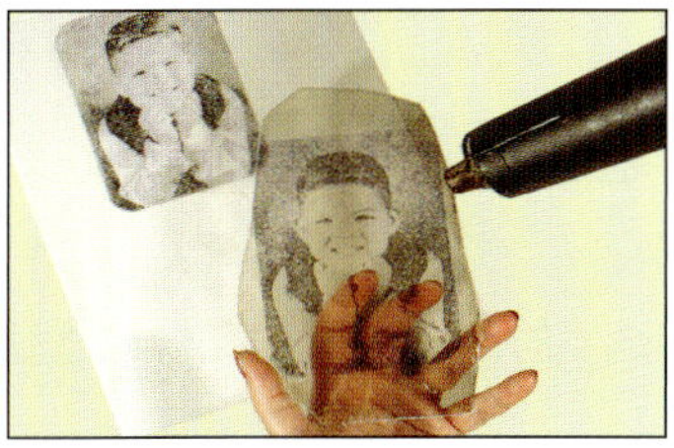

5. Dry transferred image thoroughly with a heat gun.

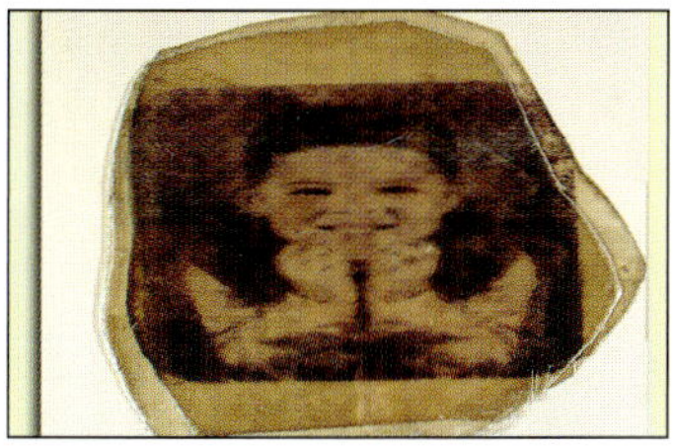

6. Carefully lay the Duo'ed tile onto the image.

Babe
by Julia Davenport

MATERIALS: *USArtQuest* (Mica Tile, PPA-Gloss, Duo Embellishing Adhesive, Soft applicator, Studio Paper, Folia cardstock: Red, Black, White) • *Dymo* labeler • *Li'l Davis* sticker letters

INSTRUCTIONS: **Card**: Cut Red cardstock 4 1/4" x 11". Fold in half to 4 1/4" x 5 1/2". • Cut Black mat 4 1/8" x 5 1/4". Cut White mat 3 3/4" x 5". Stack mats and glue to card. • **Mica**: Transfer photo to Mica Tile. Adhere tile to card. • **Finish**: Adhere label and stickers.

1965
by Frankie Fioretti

MATERIALS: *USArtQuest* (Mica Tile, PPA-Gloss, Duo Embellishing Adhesive, Soft applicator, Studio Paper, Folia cardstock: Brown, Pearl) • *Making Memories* Metal Numbers • Copper Metal Mesh • Copper Foil paper • Torn old dictionary pages • Dry embossing tool • Ruler

INSTRUCTIONS: **Card**: Cut Brown cardstock 7" x 10". Fold in half to 5" x 7". • Cut Copper foil paper mat 4" x 6". Glue to card. • **Pearl mat**: Cut Pearl paper 3 3/4" x 5 3/4". Dry emboss a rectangle 3 1/4" x 3 1/2" one half inch below top of mat. Tear pieces of an old dictionary and glue to the upper and lower corners of the mat. Glue mat to card. • **Mica**: Transfer photo to tile. Adhere tile to card inside the embossed rectangle. • **Finish**: Adhere a 1" x 3" Copper mesh and metal numbers to card.

Our scrapbook page has the nostalgic style of heirloom scrapbook pages. Note the mica image transfer is reversed.

Dance Scrapbook Page
by Julia Davenport

MATERIALS: *USArtQuest* (PPA, Large Mica Tile, Duo Embellishing Adhesive, Soft applicator, Studio Paper) • *Making Memories* (Rub-On letters, brads, photo anchors) • *Canson* photo corners • *7gypsies* paper • *Bazzill* cardstock (Dijon, Plum) • Dried flowers • Hand charm • Chocolate Brown ink • Oval punch • Hole punch

INSTRUCTIONS: **Background**: Cut text paper into 11 3/4" square. Adhere to Plum cardstock. Cut strip of Plum 3/4" x 7". Adhere to page 3" from bottom. • **Image**: Cut Plum mat 4 3/4" x 7 3/4". Cut Dijon mat 4 1/4" x 7 1/4". Cut image 4" x 7". Attach photo corners. Stack, glue image and mats together. • **Mica**: Transfer "Dance" and image to Mica Tiles. Punch word into oval shape. Punch holes in mica oval. Adhere to image mat with brads. • Glue image mat to page. • **Embellishments**: Adhere Dijon cardstock, mica scrap to page. Tear and ink edges of dance instruction paper. Glue to page. • Adhere mica image to page. Add photo anchors with brads. Glue charm and flowers in place.

This purchased lamp was already quite nice but rather ordinary. The little window shapes are ideal for this technique. Tear the white paper panels from the inside of the shade to reveal little windows.

Stained Mica

Stained mica adds yet another effect to your projects. On this lamp, stained mica replaced the shade for a stained glass look. Stained mica makes a great window for altered art and scrapbook pages. Smaller pieces are useful on cards too.

1. Select and thin mica.

2. Load the Cut n' Dry pad with Duo adhesive. Stamp onto the desired location.

3. Apply Gildenglitz foil. Carefully burnish with the Texture Sponge.

Altered Lamp

by Frankie Fioretti

MATERIALS: *USArtQuest* (Stained Mica Tiles-Grand Effects, PPA-Gloss, Duo Embellishing Adhesive, Gildenglitz, Texture Sponge) • *Ranger* 1" square Cut n' Dry ink pad • Lamp • Metal buttons • Gold embossing powder • *Tsukineko* Versamark ink pad

INSTRUCTIONS: **Mica**: Select mica large enough for one side of the lamp. Choose thicker pieces so there is enough for all sides after the mica is thinned. • Cut the pieces into panels for each side, numbering them with a Post-it note, just in case each is a slightly different size. • **Adhesive**: Load the Cut 'n Dry pad with Duo. Dab the adhesive onto the mica. On this project, the gilding falls evenly between each of the lamp windows. • **Gilding**: Let the adhesive turn clear and tacky. Add Gildenglitz foil, carefully burnishing it with the Texture Sponge. Save all the excess foil in a plastic bag. • **Finish**: Slide each panel into place. Adhere panels with PPA. • Add gold buttons for feet and lamp-top embellishments. • Emboss metal buttons with Gold. Lay the lamp on its side. Adhere buttons to the gilded square with PPA. Let dry. Turn lamp over and adhere buttons to the next panel. Let dry. Continue all around the lamp until all panels are complete.

Steven Scrapbook Page

by Frankie Fioretti

MATERIALS: *USArtQuest* (Stained Mica Tiles-Grand Effects, PPA) • *All My Memories* Earth Green Time Savers paper • Cardstock (White, Terra Cotta, Pumpkin) • *Making Memories* (Words, Foto Flips hinges) • *Stickopotamus* stickers (Leaf, Swirl) • *ColorBox* Chestnut Roan ink • Craft knife

INSTRUCTIONS: **Background**: Double-mat 3 photos with Terra Cotta and Pumpkin. Adhere 2 photos to the left side of the page. • **Title**: Computer print name, date and definitions of "grow" and "explore" on White cardstock. Cut out words. Ink the edges. Mat on Terra Cotta cardstock. Adhere name, date and stickers to left side of page. • **Mica**: Cut stained mica to cover each photo on the left side. Attach hinges to the mica. Adhere hinges to page. • **Color Blocking:** Adhere matted photo, definitions and stickers in place on right side. • **Mica**: Cut 3 strips of stained mica 1/2" x 12". Adhere 1 strip near the center of the page. • Cut 2 horizontal slits 5/8" wide in each light square just above and below each definition. Thread a mica strip through the slits and adhere at the top and bottom of the strip. • Cut 8 slits 1" in from the right edge of the page as shown. Thread mica through slits. Adhere at the top and bottom of the page.

Eyelet hinges are perfect for using a Mica Tile as a window or door. On this page, the window opens, revealing the photos underneath with greater clarity.

Stained Mica Card

by Julia Davenport

MATERIALS: *USArtQuest* (Stained Mica Tile, PPA) • Cardstock (Chocolate Brown, Tan) • Patterned paper (Beige Leaf, Black and White print) • Copper button • Gold foil paper scrap

INSTRUCTIONS: **Card**: Cut Brown cardstock 5 1/2" x 8 1/2". Fold in half to 4 1/4" x 5 1/2". • Cut Tan mat 3 3/4" x 5". Cut Leaf paper mat 3 1/2" x 4 3/4". Stack mats and glue to card. • **Mica**: Cut mica 3" x 4 1/4". Adhere to card. • **Embellishments**: Tear Black and White print 2 1/2" x 3 1/4". Adhere to card. Glue mica scrap over Black and White print. • Tear a scrap of foil paper 1 3/4" x 2". Adhere foil and Copper button to card.

Shadowboxing: Creating Dimensional Constructions

Box Lid Shadowboxing

by Frankie Fioretti

MATERIALS: *USArtQuest* (Mica Tiles, PPA) • Matboard • Foamcore • Metal corners • Decorative papers • Assorted stamps • Fibers • Metal spiral clip • Found objects for display • Craft knife • Ruler • Glue Dots

INSTRUCTIONS: **Inner box**: Cut the following matboards: **"A"** Cut 2 long sides of the box 2 3/4" x 9 3/4". **"B"** Cut 2 short sides of the box 2 3/4" x 3 1/2". **"C"** Cut 3 pieces 3 1/2" x 9 1/2" for the bottom of the inner box, underside of the lid, and top window. • Cover all box pieces with decorative paper or paint. Don't cover the lid pieces until the window is cut. Let dry. See Box Construction diagram to glue pieces together. • **Outer box**: Cut the following matboard: **"A"** Cut 2 long sides of the box 3" x 10". **"B"** Cut 2 short sides of the box 3" x 4". **"C"** From foamcore cut lid 4" x 10" and bottom 4 1/4" x 10 3/8". See Box Construction diagram to glue pieces together. • Collage bottom and assembled sides with decorative paper. Let dry. • Glue bottom to assembled sides. • Glue inner box bottom inside the box. Let dry. • Decorate sides of box with fibers as desired. • **Lid**: Cut a 2 1/2" x 6 1/4" window in the matboard lid. See lid diagram. • Place the matboard on the foamcore lid and mark a window. Cut a window in the foamcore. • Collage both pieces of the lid. • See Side View Diagram. Glue "underside of lid" to foamcore. Decorate window and adhere display objects. • **Mica**: Cut out a stamped image and glue to the underside of the mica. Add spiral clip. Glue mica over window of matboard. Add metal corners. Adhere matboard to lid with glue dots.

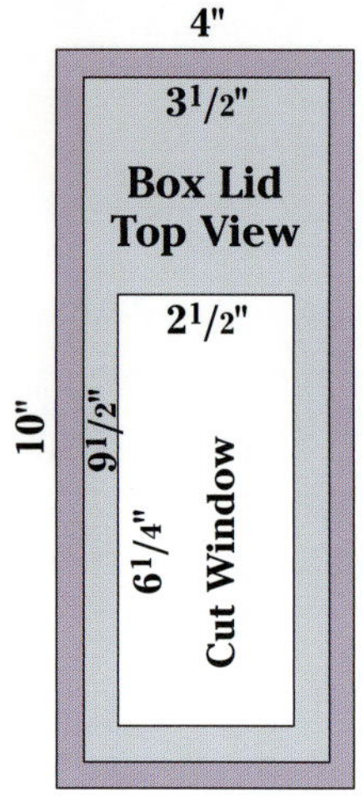

Lid Side View

Box Construction

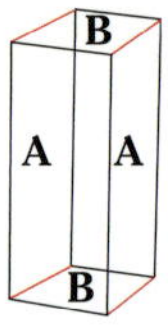

Red lines indicates where to glue seams with PPA

Photo Frame Shadowboxing

by Frankie Fioretti

MATERIALS: *USArtQuest* (Mica Tiles, PPA) • Purchased frames and mats • Metal (washers, screws, bolts) • Decorative papers • Assorted stamps • Embossing powder (Gold, Black) • Foamcore • Craft knife • Ruler

INSTRUCTIONS: **Mat**: Cut a window in the mat to desired size. Decorate mat as desired. • Adhere foamcore with PPA to the back of the mat around the window. • **Mica**: Cut mica to cover window. Drill holes in mat and mica to fit screws. Position mica and adhere it to the mat with PPA. Stack washers and add screw. Adhere with a bolt on the back of the mat. • **Inside**: Adhere decorative papers and items to frame within the window space. • **Finish**: Glue mat in position.

These boxes and frames have a sophisticated sense of style, great design, and balanced sensibility. Incorporating found objects is an artist's dream project.

Square Box with Lizard

by Frankie Fioretti

MATERIALS: *USArtQuest* (Mica Tile, Mica Flakes, Satin Mache box, Excel Board, PPA-Matte) • *Penny Black* paper • Craft knife • *Willeez* Lizard • 2" dowel • Wire • White satin ribbon 1" wide • Buttons • Fibers • *Jacquard* Lumiere paint • Gold embossing powder • *Tsukineko* Versamark ink pad • Ruler • Awl

INSTRUCTIONS: **Window**: Use a ruler to pencil in guidelines for cutting. Use a craft knife to cut the opening in the box top. • **Inside box**: Paint or collage the inside of the box. • **Embellishments**: Cut Excel board "A" to fit window and board "B" to fit snugly into the lid of the box. • **Board A**: Paint dowel with Lumiere. Wind wire around dowel. Adhere decorative papers. Emboss stamps with Gold. • Coat the lizard with PPA. Cover with mica flakes. • Affix the display elements to the board and glue a ribbon to the back so the ends extend 2" beyond the edges. • **Board B**: Decorate both sides of the board with papers and inks as desired. Adhere board "A" to the center of board "B" with the ribbon in between. • **Outer Box**: Collage, paint or otherwise embellish the outside of the box base and top. • **Mica**: Lay the mica over opening on outside of the top. Use an awl to make small starter holes. Attach buttons with fibers to hold tile in place. • **Finish**: Push board "B" into the lid so the embellishments show through the window and the ribbon tabs hang into the box.

Round Box with Keys

by Frankie Fioretti

MATERIALS: *USArtQuest* (Mica Tile, Satin Mache box, Excel Board, PPA-Matte) • *Penny Black* paper • Craft knife • Found objects • Ruler • Awl

INSTRUCTIONS: **Window**: Use a ruler to pencil in guidelines for cutting. Use a craft knife to cut the opening in box top, leaving enough clearance on the inside so the box will still close. • Cut lengths of foamcore to fit around the opening. Adhere with PPA. • Cut a piece of Excel board that will fit over the foamcore strips. • **Inside box**: Paint the inside of the top, the sides of the foamcore strips, the backside of the Excel board, and inside the box. • **Embellishments**: Glue the display elements to the unpainted side of the Excel board with PPA. Do Not embellish the edges where the board will be affixed to the foamcore strips. • Check the position of the artwork so it shows through the opening in the box top. Adhere the embellished Excel board to the foam strips. Let it dry. • **Finish**: Collage, paint or otherwise embellish the outside of the box base and top. • **Mica**: Lay the mica over the opening on the outside of the top. Use an awl to make small starter holes. Attach beads, buttons, or other small-holed items. These will also hold the tile in place.

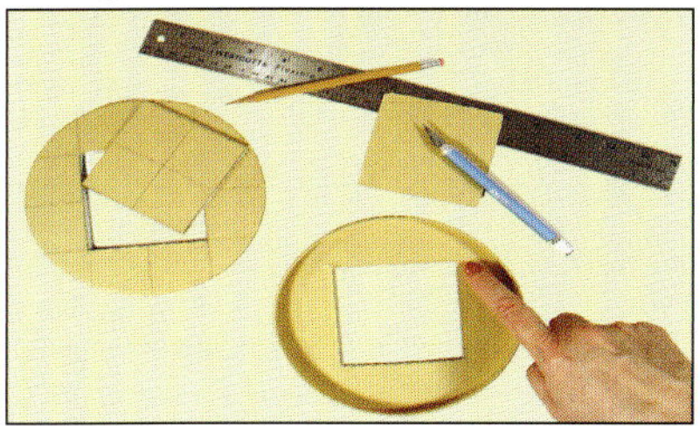

1. Draw guide lines. Cut opening in the box top.

2. Adhere the foamcore around the opening.

3. Paint the inside of the top.

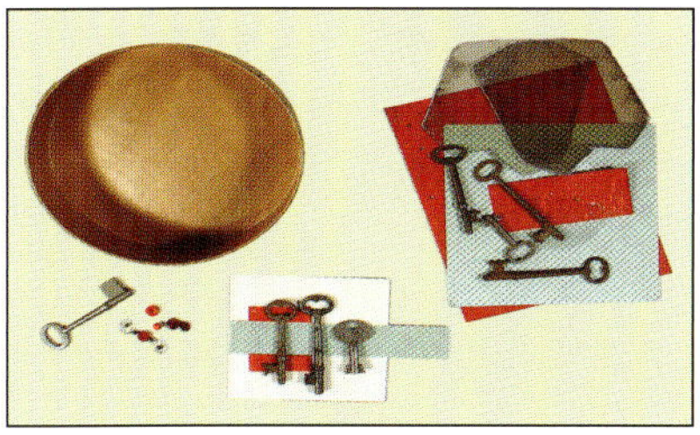

4. Affix elements to the unpainted side of the Excel board.

5. Adhere the embellished Excel board to the foam strips.

Thelma and Louise Scrapbook Page

by Susan Pickering Rothamel

This great old photo perfectly preserves the dress and hairstyles of the 40's. Take note too, of the big band on the stage in the background.

MATERIALS: *USArtQuest* (Mica, Gossamer Paper, Gilded Variegated Scrapbook Paper, PPA, Sandi Miller Art Stamp, Folia cardstock: Pale Lilac, Light Pink, Dark Brown) • *Jacquard* Piñata Colors • *Suze Weinberg* UTEE (Platinum, Copper) • *Ranger* ink (Black, White) • *Tsukineko* (Black StazOn ink, Versamark ink pad) • White embossing powder • Photo corners

INSTRUCTIONS: **Background**: Cut Gilded paper 11" x 11". Adhere to Brown cardstock. Cover with the Gossamer paper. • **Title**: Computer print the title on Light Pink cardstock. Cut out. Mat on Lilac paper. Glue to the page. • **Photo**: Cut the mats of Gilded paper and Brown. Place the corners on photo. Adhere photo to mats. Glue to the page. • **Lower left Mica**: Ink flower stamp with Black. Sprinkle Platinum UTEE onto a Mica Tile. CAUTION: To prevent burns, use a Handy Clip to hold the mica securely. Sprinkle UTEE onto mica. • Heat the mica from the underside until UTEE has melted. • Place the mica on a flat surface and impress the inked-stamp into the hot molten powder. Leave the stamp in the embossing powder for about 10 seconds. • Let cool completely. Stamp a second flower design with Black StazOn. Adhere mica to the lower corner of the page.• **Mica photo corner**: Ink the first flower stamp again. Combine Platinum and Copper UTEE on a small Mica Tile. Emboss as before. Let it cool. Adhere to the upper corner of the photo. • **Stained mica**: Cut a Mica Tile to fit the upper right corner of the page. Drizzle Piñata ink on the back of the mica. Let dry. Adhere to page. • **Friend mica**: Stamp words with Versamark. Cover with White embossing powder. Heat the powder as before. Let cool completely. Adhere mica to the page.

Relief Stamping on Mica:

Make a fabulous first impression!

Thank You Card

by Julia Davenport

This card is a true eye-catcher. The relief embossing is truly outstanding on the mica.

MATERIALS: *USArtQuest* (Mica Tile, Sandi Miller Art Stamps, Heat Gun Holster, Handy Clip, Folia cardstock: Chamois, Silver) • *Mrs. Grossman* sticker letters • Black *Colorbox* ink • *Suze Weinberg* UTEE (Platinum, Copper, Gold) • *Memory Makers* Silver brads • Heat gun • Hole punch

INSTRUCTIONS: **Card**: Cut Silver cardstock $5^1/_2$" x $8^1/_2$". Fold to $4^1/_4$" x $5^1/_2$". • **Mat**: Cut Chamois cardstock $3^3/_4$" x $4^3/_4$". • **Mica**: Ink stamp with Black. Sprinkle UTEE onto a Mica Tile. CAUTION: To prevent burns, use a Handy Clip to hold the Mica Tile securely. Sprinkle on UTEE colors. • Heat the mica from the underside until UTEE has melted. • Place the mica on a flat surface and impress the inked-stamp into the hot molten powder. Leave the stamp in the embossing powder for about 10 seconds. • Let cool to the touch. Cut the piece to fit the card. • Punch holes in the mica. Use brads to attach the mica to the Chamois mat. • **Finish**: Adhere mat to card. Place sticker in place.

1. Melt embossing powder.

2. Sprinkle mica flakes into embossing powder.

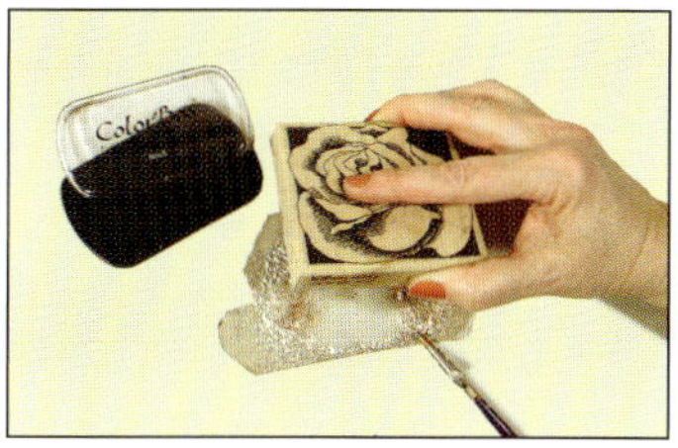

3. Ink stamp. Press stamp into the hot molten powder for 10 seconds.

4. Cut the warm mica to fit the card.

This casual country table screen is so pretty sitting in front of a window, or with a candle lit from behind. The screen itself is made of little sticks glued and nailed together. Adding charms and beads wired in the spaces is just the right finishing touch.

Table Screen

by Julia Davenport

MATERIALS: *USArtQuest* (Mica Tile-Really Big, Handy Clip, WireWorks) • *Jacquard* Pearl-Ex Jewelz • *Suze Weinberg* UTEE • *Tsukineko* Versamark ink pad • *Stampers Anonymous* stamp • *Ranger* ink • *Krylon* Gold Leafing pen • Charms • Twigs • Small finishing nails • Wood glue • Tack hammer • Hole punch

INSTRUCTIONS: See Assembly Diagram. **Twigs**: Cut 2 twigs 14 1/2" long and 1 twig 29" long. Soak twigs in water until they can be bent to shape. • Cut the following: 2 twigs 4" long, 1 twig 8 1/2" long, 3 twigs 11" long. See construction diagram Step 1. • Nail and glue bent twigs in place. • **Sides**: Cut twigs to fit for Step 3. Nail and glue to the frame from the back. • Cut twigs to fit Step 4. Add wire. Glue in place from the front. Wire charms in place.• **Center**: Cut twigs to fit center frame. Nail and glue cross pieces for Step 5. • Add decorative wires. • **Mica**: Cut mica to fit windows. Punch 4 holes in each piece of mica. • Ink the stamp. • CAUTION: Mica conducts heat. Use a Handy Clip to prevent burns. • Attach the mica to the Handy Clip. Dump UTEE on the mica in a pile. Heat from the underside. When melted, quickly stamp into the molten UTEE. Leave the stamp for 10 seconds before removing. Let it cool to the touch. Rub Jewelz over the surface. Touch the raised surfaces with a Gold leafing pen. • **Finish**: Wire the mica in place. • Wire the side frames to the middle frame loosely enough to allow the side frames to move.

Screen Construction Diagrams

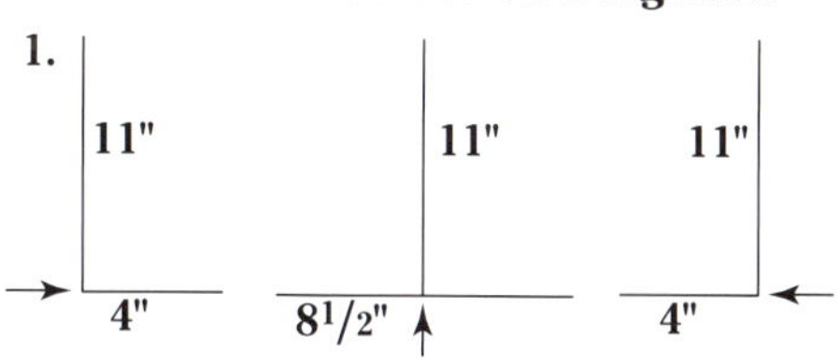

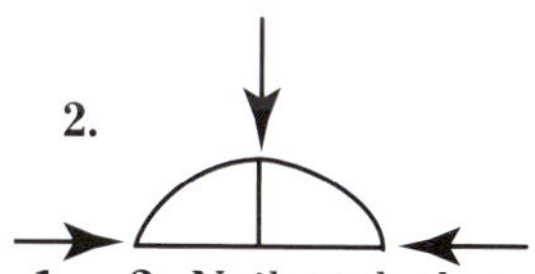

1. - 2. Nail and glue at arrows.

3. Nail from the back and glue.

4. Glue from the front.

Screen Assembly Diagram

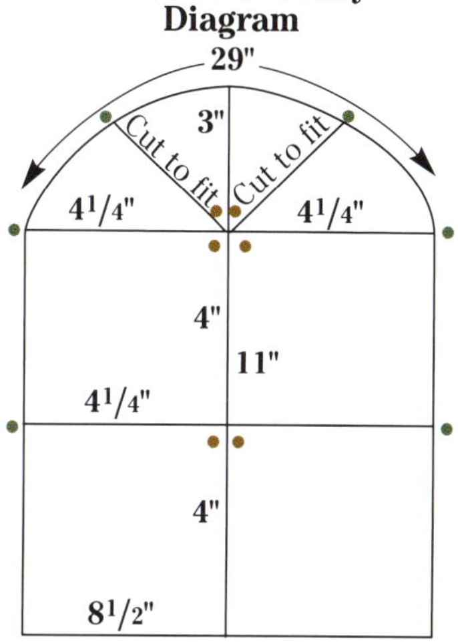

5. • Nail sticks.• Glue sticks.

Caution: *Tiles get extremely hot when heated. ALWAYS use a holder when heating a piece of mica.*

love
People say they love all kinds of things, like chocolate and movie stars, walking in the park or playing baseball. Even I say, "I love popcorn" or "I love playing in my studio". But, when it really comes down to it, and I think about what love really is, I know that love is this…this tiny little child nestled sweetly in a father's arms. There's nothing quite like seeing a Dad recognize for the very first time the fragility of his own babe. It was a near reverence on his face…and, a near panic worrying whether he would drop her. He investigated all her little fingers and toes, making sure they were all accounted for. Watching the two of them made me realize why I fell in love with him for the first time. He's a great dad already.
"I've learned that if someone says something unkind about me, I must live so that no one will believe it."

Mica Etching: Surface Effects on Mica

by Susan Pickering Rothamel

Dad & Baby Scrapbook Page

Tools suitable for etching will scratch a clean line in the mica. Tweezers will make a double line. Try using a craft knife, piercing tool, perforation wheel or upholstery needle to get the effect you want.

MATERIALS: *USArtQuest* (Mica Tiles, Mica Flakes, Tinz-Ivy, Great Tape, PPA, 101 Artist's Cement-Light, Metallic Scrapbook paper, Folia cardstock: Grass Green, White) • *Bazzill* Plum cardstock • Vellum (Printed leaves, Green) • *Cloud 9* Halo snaps • Hole punch • Needle or craft knife • Oval cutter

INSTRUCTIONS: **Background**: Cut Green Folia cardstock 11 1/2" x 11 1/2". Tape to Plum background. Cut Leaf vellum 11 3/4" x 11 3/4". Tape vellum to page so the tape will be under the mats. • **Journaling**: Print journaling on Green vellum so the words fit in a 2 1/2" x 6 3/4" space. Cut vellum 2 3/4" x 7 1/4". Cut a Plum mat 3" x 9 1/4". Cut a White mat 2 3/4" x 7". Cut a Metallic mat 1 1/2" x 2 1/2". Tape the White mat and Metallic mat to the Plum as shown in photo. Adhere Green vellum over White mat and Ivy to Metallic mat with PPA. Tape completed journaling box to page. • **Photo**: Cut Plum mat 7 1/4" x 9 1/4". Tape to page. Cut Metallic mat 6 3/4" x 8 3/4". Tape to Plum mat. • Tape photo in place. • **Mica**: Cut mica to 6" x 8". Trim off a bit of the top to make a bent line. • Use a needle or craft knife to scratch an ivy leaf pattern into each side of the mica. • Cut an oval in the mica to reveal the photo. Adhere mica flakes around the edge of the oval with 101. • Punch holes in the page and attach mica with halo snaps.

Desk Quote Frame

Stay inspired with using this quote frame, etched with your favorites and a spot to rotate new quotes inside.

MATERIALS: *USArtQuest* (Mica Tiles, PPA-Gloss) • *Jacquard* Lumiere paint • Needle or craft knife • Plastic desk frame • White paper • Paintbrush

INSTRUCTIONS **Paper Quote**: Print on White paper. Cut to fit the frame window. • **Mica**: Cut mica into pieces to create a stained glass look. • Print desired words on White paper in Black ink. • Lay mica over words. Trace with a needle or craft knife to etch. • Adhere mica to frame with PPA. • **Finish**: Paint spaces between the mica with Lumiere. Let dry. • Tape paper quote into window space.

Cherries Card

Etching or engraving produces incised or raised patterns, characters, or lines onto a surface. When using a rubber stamp as a pattern, even a novice can produce beautiful engravings. Select a stamp with a clear, clean line.

MATERIALS: *USArtQuest* (Mica Tiles, Stargazer Watercolor Palette, brush, PPA, Folia cardstock: Lemon Yellow, Fir Green, Hot Red, Pearl White) • *Rubber Stampede* Cherries stamp • *Jacquard* Gold Lumiere paint • *Tsukineko* Black StazOn ink • Etching tools • Ribbon • Fibers • Ladybug charm • Circle hole punch

INSTRUCTIONS: **Design:** Stamp onto Pearl White cardstock using permanent ink. • **Mica**: Place the mica over the stamped image and begin scribing into it with a tool. Follow the stamped lines. Occasionally check the engraving by placing it over a dark piece of paper. • **Card**: Cut a square around the cherries 3 1/2" x 3 1/2". Cut a Fir Green mat 3 5/8" x 3 5/8" and 4" x 6". Cut a Yellow mat 3 3/4" x 3 3/4" and 4 1/4" x 6 1/4". Cut a Red card 7 1/2" x 11". Fold in half to 5 1/2" x 7 1/2". • **Large Mats**: Glue Yellow and Green mats to card with PPA. Adhere etched mica to the lower corner with PPA. • **Small Mats**: Watercolor the stamped image. Layer Yellow mat, Green mat, and Cherries square with PPA. Turn at an angle and adhere to card. • **Embellishments**: Punch circles in a scrap of cardstock. Remove the circles and paint the remaining negative with Gold Lumiere. Let dry. • Thread fibers through the holes and adhere to card with PPA. Glue ladybug in place with PPA.

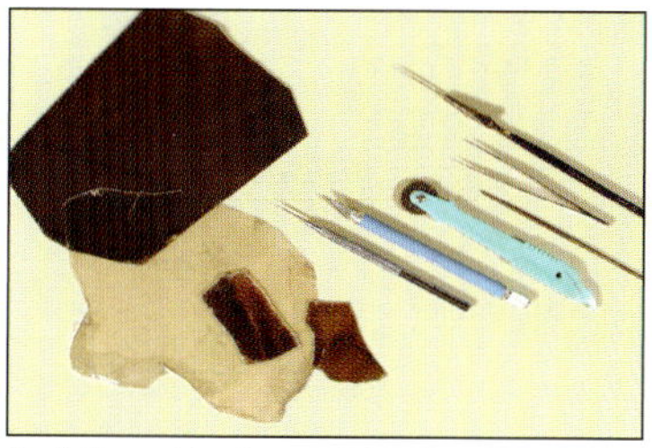

1. Mica Etching Tools

2. Stamp the permanent ink onto cardstock.

3. Lay mica over image. Etch.

4. Watercolor the original stamped image.

Grand Stamping:

Extra Large Stamps for an Extra Special Effect

This candleholder, purchased at the end of the gardening season, was the inspiration for this luminary. Always keep an eye out for easily altered home décor accessories.

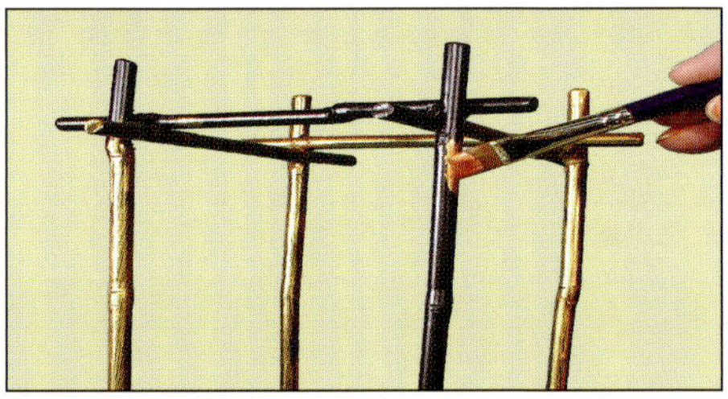

1. Paint the frame.

2. Stamp the 3 smallest mica pieces.

3. Assemble 'layers' of each decorative center.

4. Line the 3 cut sides with foil tape. Burnish the edges with a bone folder.

Luminary

by Susan Pickering Rothamel

MATERIALS: *USArtQuest* (Mica Tiles-Grand Effects, Gossamer Paper, Tinz Ivy, Great Tape, Foil-it tape) • *Fred Mullet* stamp • *Tsukineko* StazOn ink • *Jacquard* Lumiere paint • Ready-made candle frame • Hole Punch • Bone folder

INSTRUCTIONS: **Frame**: Paint the candle frame if desired. • **Mica**: Select the largest mica and thin it to make 3 panels. The back of the frame is open to light and extinguish the candle. • Each panel has a stack of 3 smaller pieces of mica in the center. Cut each a bit shorter than the next for stacking. Note: Only 3 sides of the decorative centers have been hand-cut. The top retains its natural line. • **Decorative centers**: Using StazOn ink, stamp the 3 smallest of the 9 decorative pieces. • Layer each decorative center starting at the top: stamped mica, Gossamer paper, next larger piece of mica, the biggest piece of mica, Gossamer paper. • Holding the layers firmly, line the 3 cut sides with foil tape, burnishing the edges quite firmly with a bone folder. • **Attach panels**: Line up the large panel with each side of the frame then punch the holes. If your frame does not have cross pieces, as this one does, simply set eyelets and wire attachments. Cut 12 mica 1" squares for 'washers' to fit snugly, at a diagonal, on the finished piece. • Slide each large mica panel into crossbars of the frame. Apply a touch of adhesive and glue the square mica washers to the large mica. If your frame has no cross pieces, wire it into place. • **Finish**: Use the tape or gloss adhesive to affix each decorative mica center to the panel. Embellish the luminary using bits of Copper ivy or other decorative accent of your choice.

Fish Wall Hanging

by Susan Pickering Rothamel

MATERIALS: *USArtQuest* (Mica Tiles-Grand Effects, PPA, Great Tape) • Woodgrain print paper • *Fred Mullet* Large Fish stamp • *Ranger* Cut n' Dry ink pad • *Jacquard* Neopaque paint (Black, Russet) • Washers • Wire • Hole punch • Eyelets • Eyelet tools • Beads • Tassel • Black cord • Picture frame • Bamboo sticks • Tack hammer • Small finishing nails

INSTRUCTIONS: **Paint**: Paint 2 washers and bamboo with Russet. Let dry. • **Mica**: Delaminate several pieces of mica. Trim if needed. Space them to fit the frame. • Apply Black paint to Cut n' Dry pad. Stamp on mica. Let dry. • **Washers**: Punch holes in mica and adhere painted washers over holes, front and back. • **Assembly**: String the bamboo together with wire. Set eyelets in mica. Wire mica to bamboo. Attach the bamboo to the top and bottom of the frame. • **Paper**: Turn the piece over and place Great Tape on the edges of the frame. Place the woodgrain paper over the back of the frame, sealing the edges on all 4 sides. Trim any excess paper. • **Finish**: Tack on decorative tassel and cord to hang the piece.

Large stamps create bold images. The rattan sticks, colors and beautiful woodgrain art paper give this piece a decidedly Asian feeling.

Every flower garden should have such charming tags! Use the seed package designs and everyone will know which seeds have been planted, or create your own.

Mica Encapsulation: Window Garden Delights

1. Die-cut a mica tag. Delaminate to get two mica pieces for each package of seeds you use.

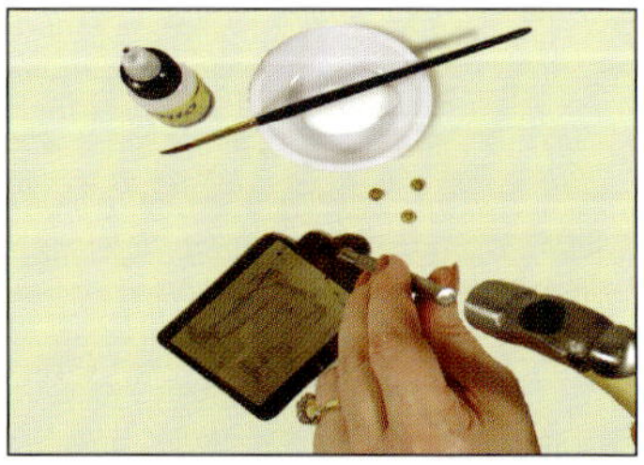

2. Set an eyelet at the top of each tag.

Garden Pot Stakes

by Shawn Hall and Susan Pickering Rothamel

MATERIALS: *USArtQuest* (Duo Embellishing Adhesive, brush) • Seed Package labels • Die-Cut tags to fit the label • Eyelets • Eyelet tools • Lightweight wire coat hanger • Wire cutters • Pliers • Copper acrylic paint

INSTRUCTIONS: **Tag**: Die-cut tags that fit the seed packages. Delaminate each tag to yield at least 2 mica pieces for each seed package. • Apply Duo to 1 side of each mica tag. Let dry until tacky. • Sandwich the seed package between the mica tags. Set an eyelet at the top of each tag. • **Hanger**: Cut and shape a wire hanger plant stake for each seed tag. Paint the hangers Copper. • **Assembly**: Thread the tag from the bottom of the stake so it hangs freely. Plant the stake in a pot.

3. Cut and shape a wire stake for each seed tag.

4. Thread the tag on the stake so that it hangs freely.

Mica Texture: From Fragments to Fish Scales

by Julia Davenport

The antique pearl-colored mica is beautiful, used as an embellishment or embedded in paper. For this technique the pearlescent quality also gives transparent permanent inks a radiance not easily duplicated on clear plastic or acetate.

Turquoise Fish Art

MATERIALS: *USArtQuest* (Perfect fx Mica Flakes-Antique Pearl, Tinz Fish, PPA, 101 Artist's Cement-Light, Scrapbook paper-Metallic, Silver Excel board, Sandi Miller Art Stamps, Folia cardstock: Sky Blue, Middle Blue, Pacific Blue) • *Jacquard* Piñata colors • Palette Knife • Turquoise button for the eye • Turquoise matboard • Turquoise ink pad

INSTRUCTIONS: **Fish**: Use a palette knife to cover fish liberally with 101. Embed the flakes at an angle. Place a button for the eye. Finish embedding the mica. Let dry. • Apply White ink all over the surface, except the eye. • Drizzle several Piñata colors over the surface. Let dry. • **Large Mat**: Cut Turquoise mat 5" x 6 1/4". Cut Middle Blue cardstock 4 1/4" x 5 1/2". Cut Sky Blue mat 3 3/4" x 5". Stamp the Sky Blue mat with "Wild" and "Free" in Turquoise ink. • Layer mats. Glue in place with PPA. • **Small mat**: Cut Metallic paper mat 2 5/8" x 3 3/4". Cut Excel board 2 3/8" x 3 1/4". Cut Pacific Blue cardstock 2 1/8" x 3". • Layer mats. Adhere to large mat with PPA. • **Finish**: Adhere fish to mat with 101.

Fragment Box

MATERIALS: *USArtQuest* (Perfect fx Mica Flakes-Antique Pearl, Satin Mache box, 101 Artist's Cement-Light) • *Jacquard* (Piñata colors, Purple Lumiere paint) • Palette Knife •

INSTRUCTIONS: **Box**: Paint the box and inside lid with Purple. Let dry. • **Lid**: Use a palette knife to cover the lid liberally with 101. Embed the flakes at an angle. Let dry. • Apply White ink all over the surface. • Drizzle several Piñata colors over the surface. Let dry.

Red Fish Art

MATERIALS: *USArtQuest* (Perfect fx Mica Flakes-Antique Pearl, Tinz Fish, PPA, 101 Artist's Cement-Light, Excel board: Copper, White • Sandi Miller Art Stamps, Folia cardstock: Ochre, Brick Red, Dark Red, Hibiscus) • *Jacquard* Piñata colors • Palette Knife • Red button for the eye • Red ink pad • *Krylon* Copper Leafing pen

INSTRUCTIONS: **Fish**: See directions for Turquoise fish. • **Large Mat**: Cut White mat and Ochre cardstock 5" x 6 1/4". Cut Brick Red cardstock 4 1/4" x 5 1/2" and 3 3/4" x 5". Stamp the smaller Brick Red mat with fish in Red ink. Edge mat with Copper leafing pen. • Layer mats. Glue in place with PPA. • **Small mat**: Cut Dark Red mat 2 7/8" x 3 3/4". Cut Hibiscus mat 2 3/4" x 3 5/8". Cut 3 pieces of Copper Excel board 1" x 2 1/2". • Layer mats. Adhere to large mat with PPA. • **Finish**: Adhere fish to mat with 101.

1. Select the shape. Cover with 101. Embed mica flakes at an angle. Place an eye. Add more mica flakes.

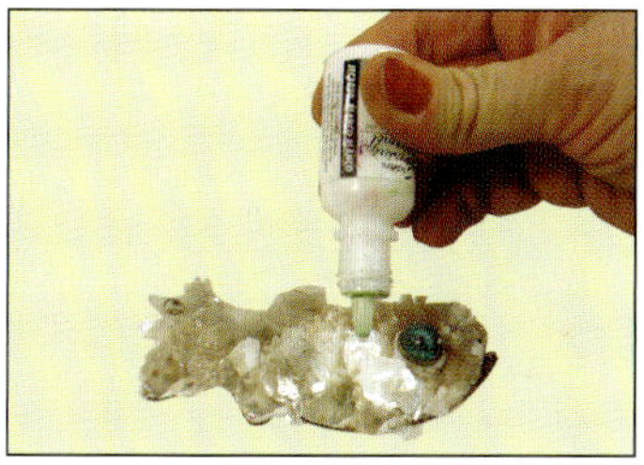

2. Except for the eye, cover the surface with White ink.

3. Drizzle ink over the surface. Let dry.

4. Mount the fish onto a layered paper surface.

Birdhouse Clock

by Susan Pickering Rothamel

MATERIALS: *USArtQuest* (Mica Tiles-Regular, Perfect fx Mica Flakes, Tinz ivy, Gildenglitz, 101 Artist Cement-Heavy, PPA-Gloss) • Purchased paper mache birdhouse • Ceramic (Beads, Buttons) • Twigs • Paper clock face • Clock fittings • Decorative papers • Black waxed linen • *Jacquard* Copper Lumiere paint • Black paint • Paintbrush • Craft knife • Hole punch

INSTRUCTIONS: **Birdhouse**: Use a craft knife to remove 1 side of the birdhouse to make a door. • **Collage**: Paint and collage entire birdhouse and door as desired. • **Mica**: Paint the areas to be covered by Mica Tile Black. Let dry. • Cover Black area with PPA. Sprinkle mica flakes. Adhere Mica Tile. • **Door**: Punch holes in the door and house to match for lacing the door to the house. • Adhere clock face to door. • Follow manufacturer's instructions to attach clock works. • Lace door to box with waxed linen. • **Roof**: Paint roof Copper. Adhere twigs with 101. Sprinkle with mica flakes while the 101 is still wet. Add ceramic buttons as desired.

Picture Frame

by Julia Davenport

MATERIALS: *USArtQuest* (Mica Tiles-Regular, Perfect fx-Crystal Shimmer Mica Flakes, PPA-Gloss) • *Krylon* Silver Leafing pen • *Jacquard* (Pearl-Ex Jewelz, Piñata colors, Extender) • Cardstock frame or ready-made mat • Sponge • Purchased photo frame • Fine brush

INSTRUCTIONS: **Frame**: Sponge Piñata ink 1 color at a time onto the frame. Use plenty of extender to blend the edges of the colors. • **Mica**: Cut and arrange mica pieces around the frame as desired. Edge each piece of mica with the Silver pen. • Adhere mica to frame with PPA. Let dry. • Use a fine brush to paint the spaces between the mica with PPA. While wet, sprinkle in the Perfect fx. • **Finish**: Mat a small piece of art or photo in the center of the frame.

1. Sponge one color at a time onto the frame.

2. Edge the mica with gilding pen.

3. Adhere the mica to the frame. Let dry.

Mica Mosaics: Beautiful Mosaic Tile Effects

Tile Table

by Susan Pickering Rothamel

This accent table covered in Mica Tiles, mica flakes and gild is truly stunning.

MATERIALS: *USArtQuest* (Mica Tiles-Regular, Perfect fx Mica Flakes, Gildenglitz, Duo Embellishing Adhesive, PPA-Gloss) • Purchased table • *PSX* rubber stamp • *Tsukineko* StazOn ink (Black, Brown) • Paintbrush • Polyurethane sealant

INSTRUCTIONS: **Mica**: Cut mica pieces and arrange them in a mosaic pattern. Adhere mica to table with PPA. • Brush PPA in the spaces between the mica. While wet, sprinkle Perfect fx and Gildenglitz. Let dry. • Stamp the gilded areas with permanent ink. • **Finish**: Coat the table with polyurethane sealant. Let dry.

Colorful and easy, our mosaic frame displays a beautifully made woven polymer clay motif.

4. Paint spaces with PPA. While wet, sprinkle Crystal Shimmer Perfect fx.

Mica Mosaics

This table tray is both practical and attractive. If you need a smaller project using the same technique, check out the picture frame.

Table Tray

by Julia Davenport

MATERIALS: *USArtQuest* (Mica Tiles-Regular, Perfect fx Mica Flakes, PPA-Gloss) • Paper mache tray • Black drawer pulls • Black paint • Paintbrush • Polyurethane sealant

INSTRUCTIONS: **Tray**: Paint the tray Black. **Mica**: Cut mica pieces and arrange them in a mosaic pattern. Adhere mica to tray with PPA. • Brush PPA in the spaces between the mica. While wet, sprinkle Perfect fx. Let dry. • **Assembly**: Coat the tray with polyurethane sealant. Let dry. • Attach drawer pulls.

Picture Frame

by Susan Pickering Rothamel

MATERIALS: *USArtQuest* (Mica Tiles-Regular, Perfect fx Mica Flakes, PPA-Gloss) • Black journal covers with binding holes • Bamboo skewers • Cardstock (Red, Gray) • Paintbrush • 4 Red mini brads • Red paint

INSTRUCTIONS: **Mica**: Cut mica pieces and arrange them in a mosaic pattern on the inside of the journal covers. Adhere mica with PPA. • Brush PPA in the spaces between the mica. While wet, sprinkle Perfect fx. Let dry. • **Mats**: Cut a Gray and Red mat to layer behind the photo. Glue mats together with PPA. Adhere photo to mat with brads. Glue mats inside each cover. • **Assembly**: Cut a 2" long bamboo skewer for every binder hole. • Paint bamboo skewers Red. Let dry. Place skewers into binder holes. Glue skewers in place with PPA.

1. Use gloss adhesive to adhere flowers and leaves.

The water glass effect works beautifully on Mica Tiles as well as glass and plastic. Nearly any clear surface can be easily altered using this technique.

Table Screen

by Susan Pickering Rothamel

MATERIALS: *USArtQuest* (Mica Tiles-Grand Effects, Perfect fx Mica Flakes, Pressed Flowers, PPA-Gloss, Texture Sponge) • Craft knife • Cutting board • Black Poster Framing Strips/Scroll Mounts (2 per panel) • Very small tubes, coffee stir straws, sticks or ready-made hinges

INSTRUCTIONS: **Mica**: Select mica to fit the screen and delaminate it to the number of panels that you would like. There are five panels on this screen. Each mica panel is 5" x 10". Two extra panels are made expressly to fracture to create added dimension. • Use PPA to adhere the flowers and leaves in a pleasing motif. While adhesive is still wet, sprinkle in natural colors of mica flakes. Let dry. • Use the texture sponge to pounce on PPA. For a more dramatic effect, use more adhesive or apply a second coat. Let dry. • Cut strips of stained mica for top and bottom borders. • **Assembly**: First, lay the complete screen on a table surface. Slide the mica strips and panels into the framing. Use more adhesive to seal the edges, both front and back, so the panels and strips don't slip. • Use ready-made hinges or make your own by adhering the tubes to the framing material and sliding in the pin.

2. Sprinkle mica flakes while the adhesive is wet. Let dry.

3. Use a Texture Sponge to pounce on PPA-Gloss.

4. Slide the strips and panels into the framing.

5. Attach the panels with hinges. See materials.

Postage Stamps as Artwork

Easy and dramatic, this necklace can be worn or hung as an accessory in your bedroom or bath.

Image Necklace

by Susan Pickering Rothamel

MATERIALS:

USArtQuest (Regular or Really Big Mica Tile, Great Tape) • *Art Accents* Postals • Art paper • Eyelets • Beads • Post earring • Polymer clay • Eyelet tools • Wire Cutters • Pliers

INSTRUCTIONS:

Tools: Select the tools and items to create the necklace. • **Mica**: Sandwich decorative paper and the postage stamp between 2 Mica Tiles. Tape the edges of the mica together. • Position 4 small eyelets to hold the Mica Tiles together and make the openings to thread the necklace cord. • **Earring**: Use wire cutters to trim off MOST of the post, leaving enough post to go through 2 Mica Tiles. Make a small round polymer clay button to cover the pointed end. • **Necklace**: Thread the cord through necklace. Knot cord on the backside and touch the knots with adhesive. Also, use the adhesive to glue the polymer button to the end of the earring post.

1. Select the tools and items to create the necklace.

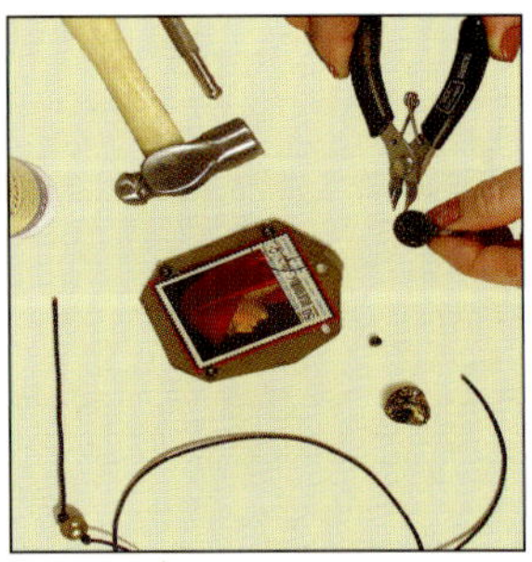

2. Use wire cutters to trim off MOST of the post. Leave behind just enough to go through two Mica Tiles.

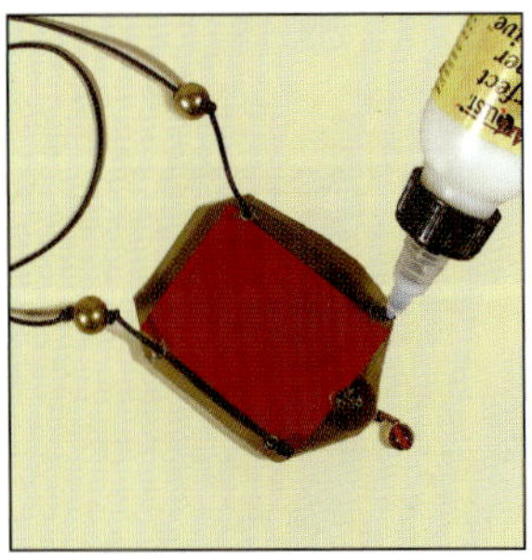

3. Knot the cord from the backside and touch the knots with adhesive.

Susan Pickering Rothamel

Susan, founder and president of USArtQuest, Inc., began her career as a graphic artist, then turned fine artist, working with oils, collage and enamel.

Susan's accomplishments include internationally distributed video workshops and national lecture tours.

Her books include 'The Art of Paper Collage', and the 'Encyclopedia of Scrapbooking'. She also writes freelance and editorially for several national magazines and publications.

Julia Davenport

Julie began her career working at USArtQuest after graduating with a BA in art. She loves exploring just about every conceivable art form, from stamping, scrapping and writing to product development, organizing classes and marketing.

Frankie Fioretti

Frankie's life is filled with art, creative materials and a love of all things pleasing to the eye. She has won acclaim as an instructor, as well as a marketing consultant to stores. She encourages shop owners to explore possibilities with art products in order to inspire their students.

SUPPLIERS - Most craft and variety stores carry an excellent assortment of supplies. If you need something special, ask your local store to contact the following companies.

USARTQUEST, 517-522-6225, www.usartquest.com
7800 Ann Arbor Rd. Grass Lake, MI 49240
AccuCut, 800-288-1670, Fremont, NE
Bazzill, 480-558-8557, Gilbert, AZ
ColorBox, 800-448-4862, Anacortes, WA
Ellison, 800-253-2238, Lake Forest, CA
Hero Arts, 800-822-4376, Emeryville, CA
Jacquard, 800-442-0455, Healdsburg, CA
Magic Scraps, 972-238-1838, Richardson, TX
McGill, 800-982-9884, Marengo, IL
PSX, 800-782-6748, Santa Rosa, CA
Ranger, 800-244-2211, Tinton Falls, NJ
Rubber Stampede, 800-632-8386, Whittier, CA
Stampers Anonymous,
440-250-9112, West Lake, OH
Tsukineko, 800-769-6633,Redmond, WA
Suze Weinberg, 732-761-2400, Freehold, NJ

MANY THANKS to my friends for their cheerful help and wonderful ideas!
Kathy McMillan • Jennifer Laughlin
Patty Williams • Marti Wyble
Donna Kinsey
David & Donna Thomason